STEP-by-STEP

GEOGRAPHY

Maps and Globes

Sabrina Crewe

Illustrated by Raymond Turvey and Shirley Tourret

CHILDREN'S PRESS®

A Division of Grolier Publishing

LONDON • NEW YORK • HONG KONG • SYDNEY
DANBURY, CONNECTICUT

© 1996 Franklin Watts

First American Edition 1997 by

Children's Press

A Division of Grolier Publishing

Sherman Turnpike

Danbury, CT 06816

ISBN: 0 516 20236 7

Library of Congress Cataloging-in-Publication Data

Crewe, Sabrina

Maps and Globes/Sabrina Crewe; illustrated by Raymond Turvey and Shirley Tourret

p. cm. -- (Step-by-step geography)

Includes index.

Summary: An introduction to maps, globes, and how to use them.

1. Maps--juvenile literature. 2. Globes--juvenile literature. [1. Maps. 2. Globes.]

I. Turvey, Raymond, ill. II. Tourret, Shirley, illus. III. Title. IV. Series.

GA105.6.C74 1997

912--dc20   96-20091

CIP AC

Printed in Dubai

Planning and production by The Creative Publishing Company

Designed by Ian Winton

Edited by Patience Coster

Consultant: Keith Lye

Photographs: The Image Bank: page 5 (Stephen Wilkes); NASA: page 25; Robert Harding Picture Library: page 28 (Mike Agliolo); Tony Stone Worldwide: page 20 (John Lawrence); ZEFA: page 24.

Contents

What Are Maps? 4

Making a Plan 6

Symbols and Keys 8

Using Colors 10

Which Direction? 12

Following a Route 14

Where Am I? 16

How Far Is It? 18

Maps for Different Things 20

City Maps 22

How Maps Are Made 24

Atlases 26

Special Maps 28

Maps and Globes 30

Glossary 32

Index 32

What Are Maps?

Maps are drawings of places, seen from above. Imagine you are in an airplane, flying over your house. You can see where your house is in the street. You can also see the other streets and houses near where you live.

Maps can show a big **area**, such as a whole town or country, on a small piece of paper. They tell us where things are and help us find our way. This is a map of the streets in the picture on page 4.

PARK STREET

ORCHARD ROAD

POND STREET

Maps can show us the whole world, too. A round map of the world is called a **globe**. Globes show us how the world looks from a spaceship.

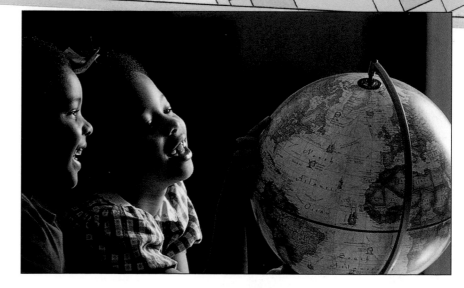

Making a Plan

Try making a **plan** of something you know, like your table at home or at school.

Look at the things on this table. You can see them all outlined in the plan below the picture.

The plan is a map of the table. It shows where everything is.

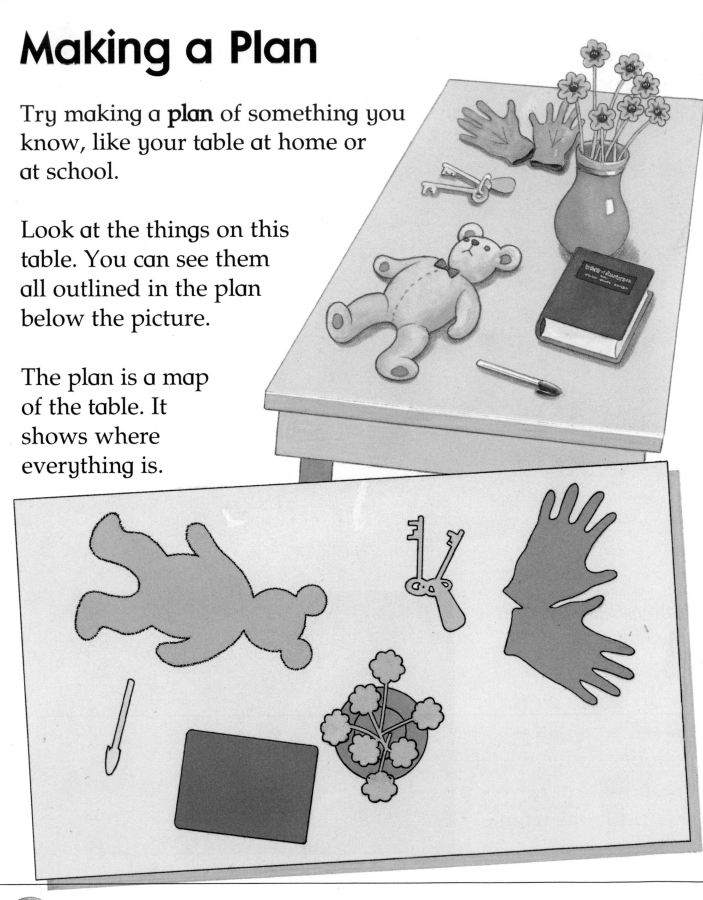

You could make a map of your room to show a friend. Remember that a map is a picture drawn from above. First draw the shape of the room. Then mark where the door and windows are. Now put in your bed and the other furniture.

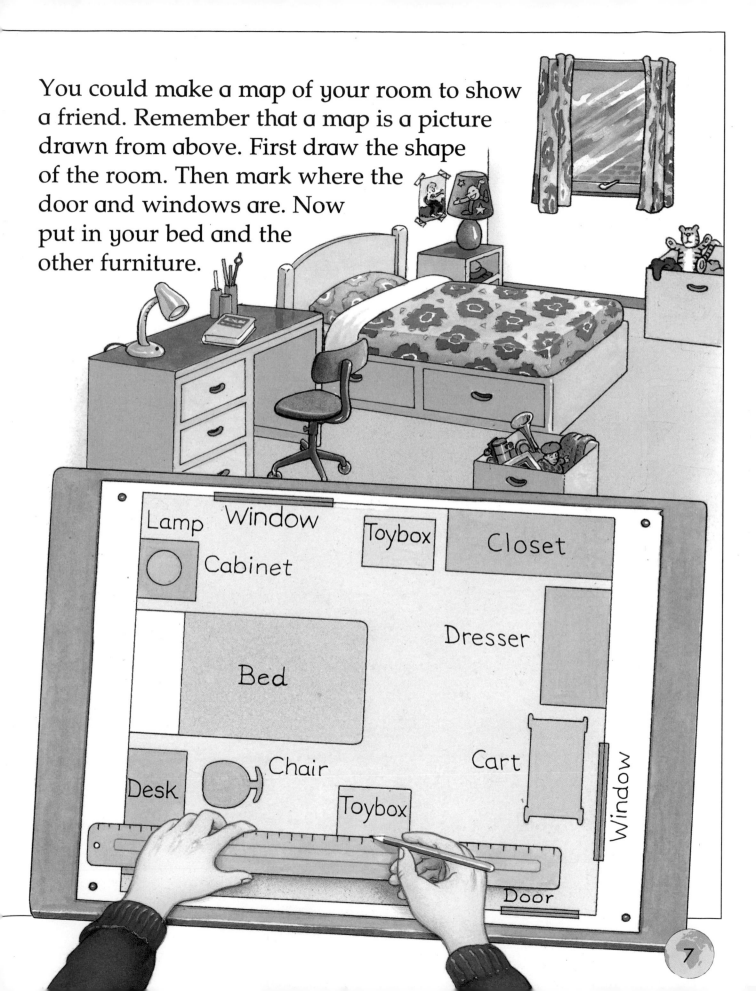

Window

Lamp

Cabinet

Toybox

Closet

Bed

Dresser

Desk

Chair

Cart

Toybox

Door

Window

Symbols and Keys

Symbols are little signs on a map. Many maps use symbols to show where things are.

On this map, the purple symbols stand for stores. The grey lines are roads. The blue wavy line is a river. All of these are symbols. What other symbols can you see?

The list on the side of the map is called a "key." This tells you what the symbols mean. What do you think the knife-and-fork symbol is for?

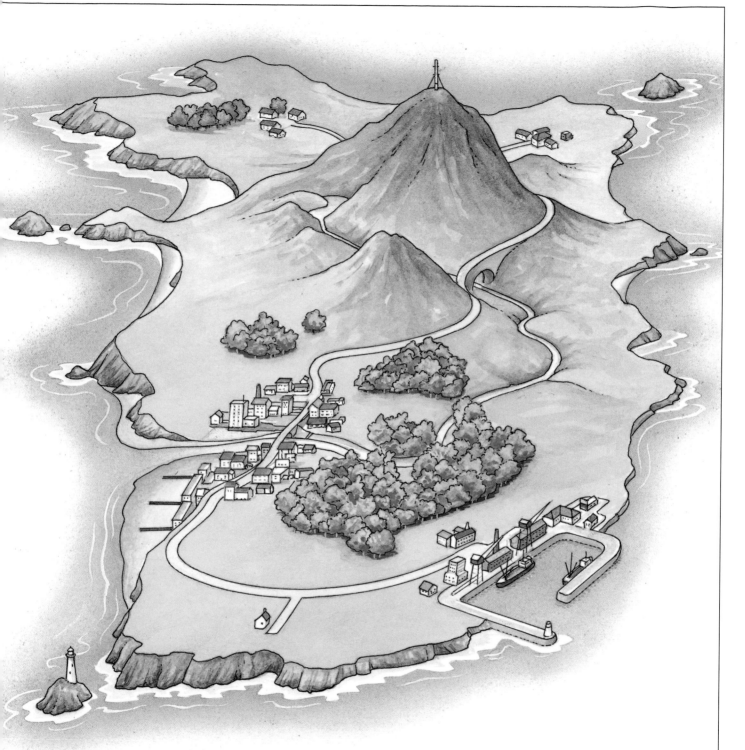

Draw a map of an island like the one in this picture. Think about the things you can see on the island. What symbols would you use to show these things? Make a key with symbols for your island map.

Using Colors

Look at this map of a park. Colors are used to show what the different parts are.

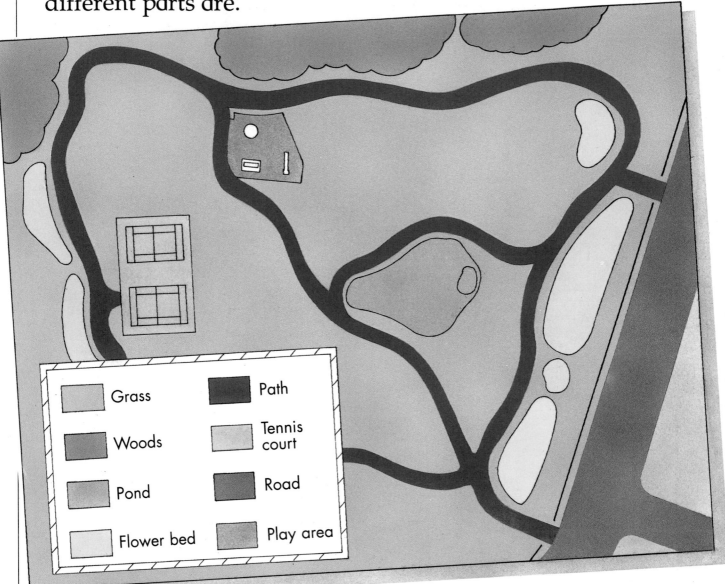

The key tells us that the light green areas are grass and the dark green areas are woods. Blue is used for the pond and pink for the play area. Look in the key for more colors. What do yellow and red stand for?

Make a map of your garden, or a park near you, using colors to show what things are.

On this tourist map, colors and symbols are used together. The colors show where the land and sea are. The symbols show us places that are fun to visit.

Castle
Church
Stores
Museum
View point
Place of interest
Water sports
Forest
Hills
Beach
Funfair
Public beach

Which Direction?

While a map can tell you where things are, you also need to know which **direction** to travel in. We go in different directions to get to different places. There are four main directions: north, south, east, and west.

This is a **compass**. It tells you which direction you are facing. A compass has a needle that always points north. If you face north too, then south is behind you; west is on your left, and east is on your right.

MAKE A COMPASS

1 Ask an adult to help you with this project. Stroke a sewing needle with a magnet about 50 times. Stroke the needle in the same direction each time. This will make the needle magnetic.

2 Cut a circle of thin cardboard. Balance the needle on this and float it in a saucer of water. The needle will move around until it points north.

Maps are usually made with north at the top and south at the bottom. Imagine you are on the bridge in this map. Which direction would you go to get to the mountain? If the farmer's dog is by the pond, which direction must it go to get back to the farm?

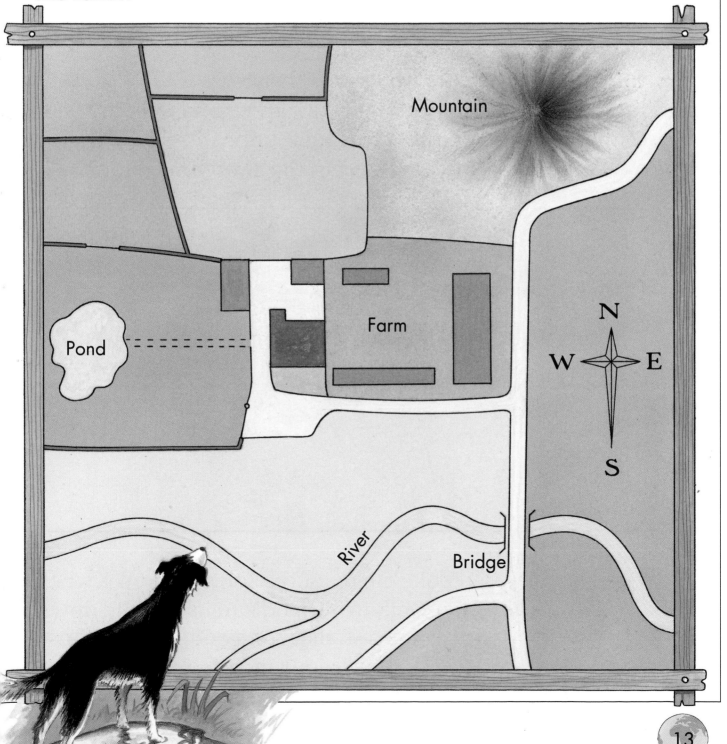

Mountain

Pond

Farm

N
W   E
S

River

Bridge

Following a Route

We all use a route to get to the places we want to go.

Vicky lives at 21 Cherry Tree Lane. Ben has asked Vicky around to his house at 4 Willow Drive. To get there, Vicky turns left out of her gate and right at the end of the lane into Park Street. She walks past the stores and turns left at the library into High Street. She passes the playground then turns right into Willow Drive. Ben's house is next to the church.

Make a map of the route you take when you walk to a friend's house. Write down directions so that someone else could use your map to find their way.

Somewhere on this map there is some buried treasure.
Can you find it? Follow the directions
to the secret hiding place.

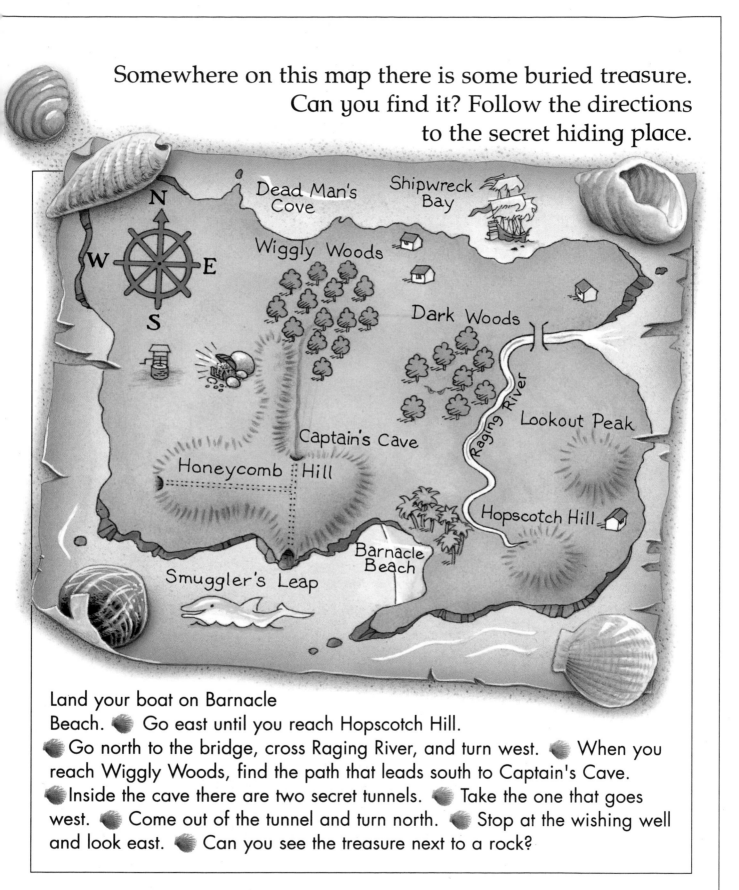

Land your boat on Barnacle
Beach. 🐚 Go east until you reach Hopscotch Hill.
🐚 Go north to the bridge, cross Raging River, and turn west. 🐚 When you
reach Wiggly Woods, find the path that leads south to Captain's Cave.
🐚 Inside the cave there are two secret tunnels. 🐚 Take the one that goes
west. 🐚 Come out of the tunnel and turn north. 🐚 Stop at the wishing well
and look east. 🐚 Can you see the treasure next to a rock?

Where Am I?

Some maps have lines that cross each other to form squares. These squares make a **grid**. A grid is very useful if you want to tell somebody exactly where to look on a map. Each square can be named by a letter and a number.

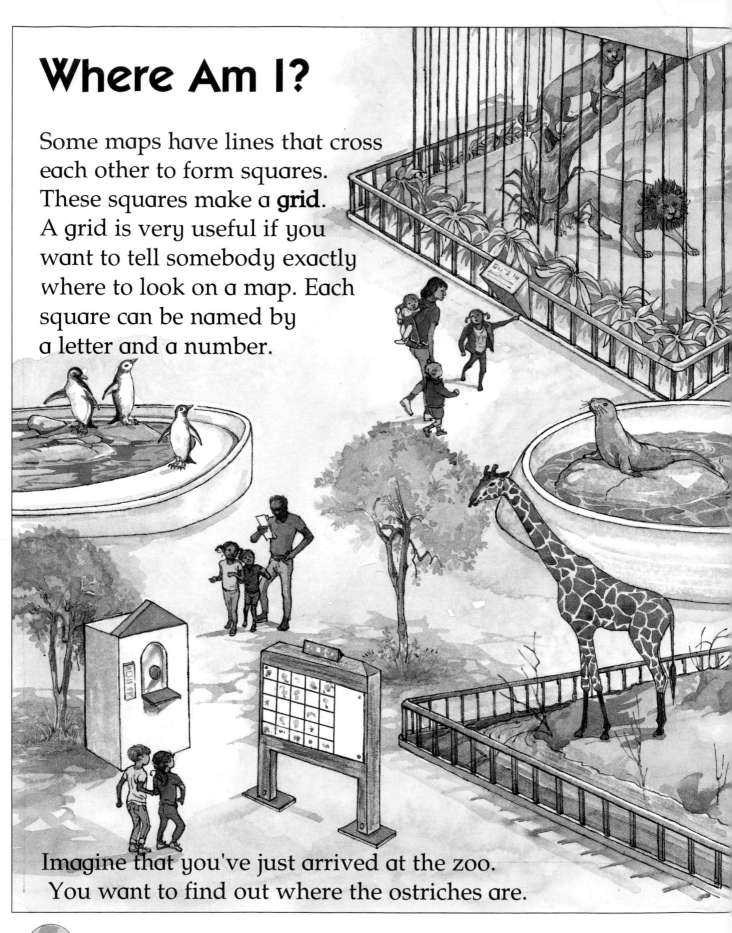

Imagine that you've just arrived at the zoo. You want to find out where the ostriches are.

If you look at the key, you'll find that the ostriches are in square **B2**. Put one finger on the letter **B** at the side of the map. Now put another finger on the number **2** at the top. Bring your fingers together in straight lines until they meet at the ostriches.

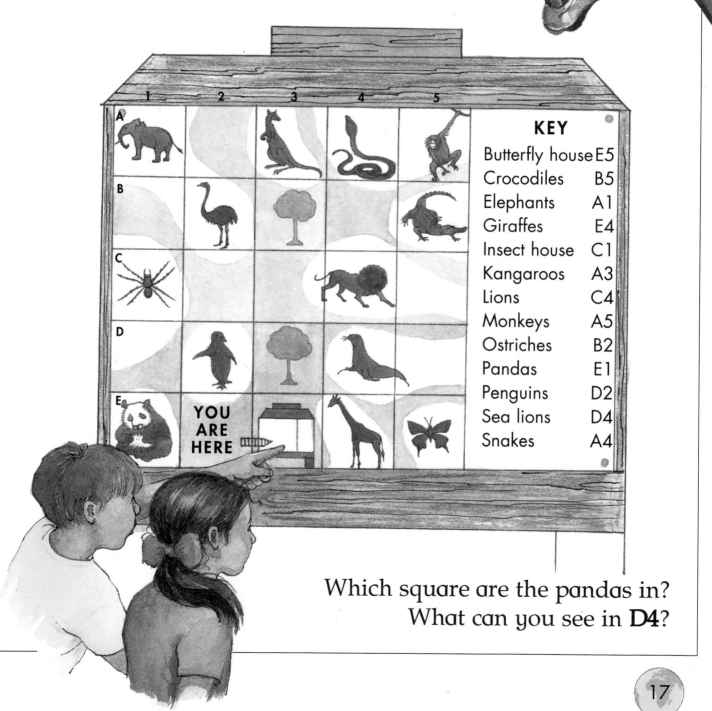

KEY

Butterfly house	E5
Crocodiles	B5
Elephants	A1
Giraffes	E4
Insect house	C1
Kangaroos	A3
Lions	C4
Monkeys	A5
Ostriches	B2
Pandas	E1
Penguins	D2
Sea lions	D4
Snakes	A4

YOU ARE HERE

Which square are the pandas in?
What can you see in **D4**?

How Far Is It?

Maps are much smaller than the places they show. But they can still tell you the real size and **distance**. The places shown on maps would not fit life-size on to a piece of paper, so maps are always drawn to **scale**.

Most maps have a **scale bar** so that you can figure out how big things are and what the distance between them is.

Garden

Castle

Orchard

This is a large scale map. You can see a castle and a garden. The scale bar shows us that half an inch on this map is 30 feet in real life. What is the distance in feet from the castle gate to the orchard?

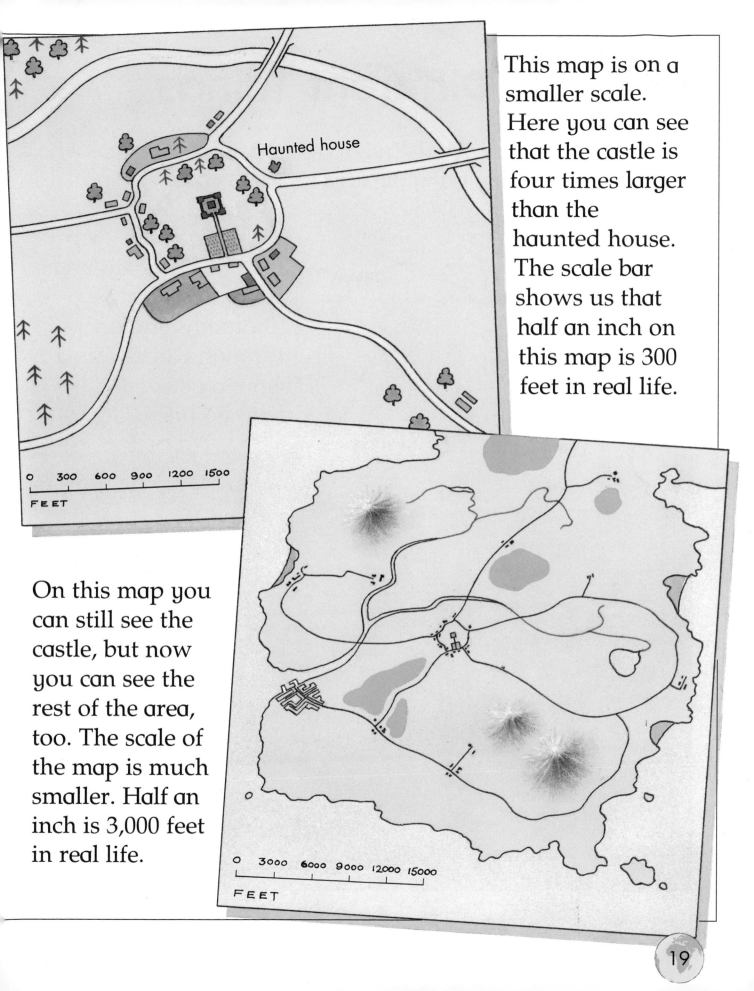

Haunted house

0   300   600   900   1200   1500

FEET

This map is on a smaller scale. Here you can see that the castle is four times larger than the haunted house. The scale bar shows us that half an inch on this map is 300 feet in real life.

On this map you can still see the castle, but now you can see the rest of the area, too. The scale of the map is much smaller. Half an inch is 3,000 feet in real life.

0   3000   6000   9000   12000   15000

FEET

Maps for Different Things

This is a walking map. It is full of information for people who are interested in exploring the area on foot.

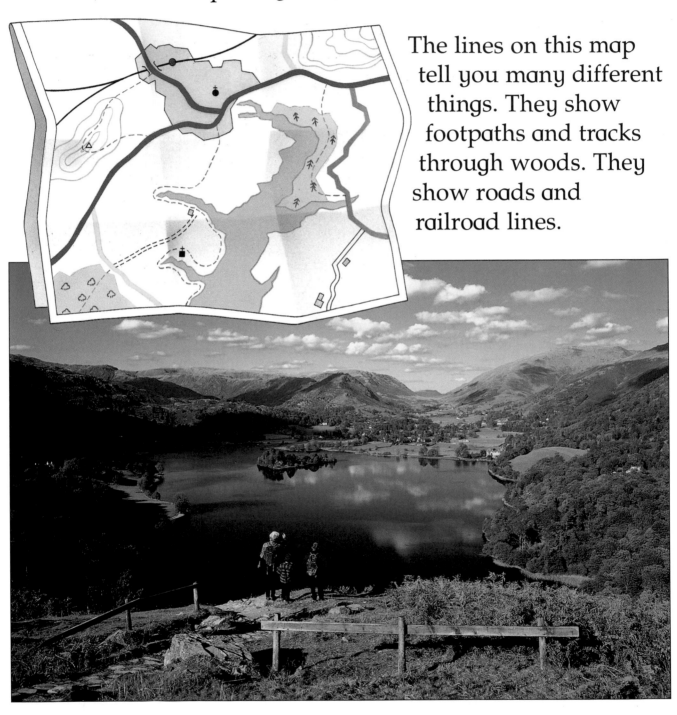

The lines on this map tell you many different things. They show footpaths and tracks through woods. They show roads and railroad lines.

The red lines on this map of South America cannot be seen in real life. They mark the **boundaries** between countries. This map doesn't help you to get around, but it is very useful for learning about other places in the world.

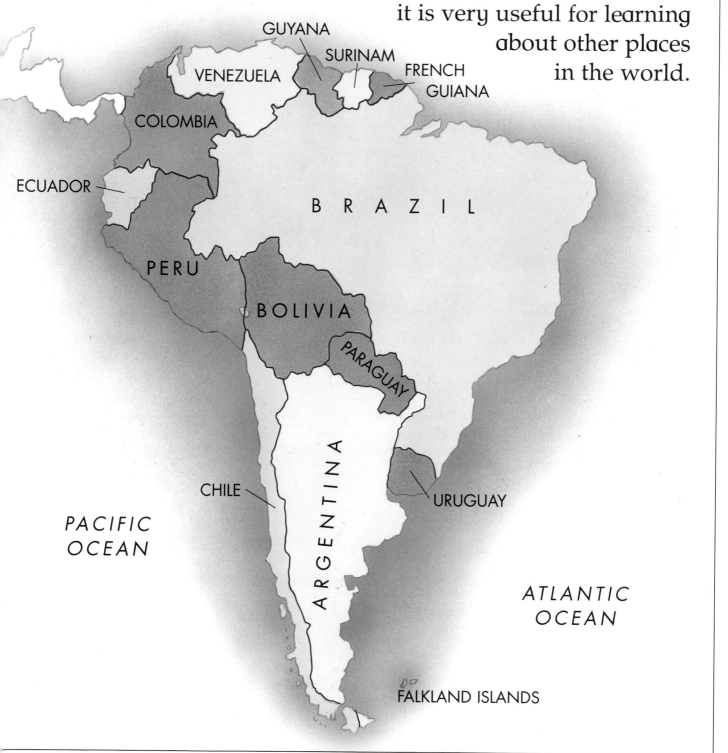

GUYANA

SURINAM

VENEZUELA

FRENCH GUIANA

COLOMBIA

ECUADOR

B R A Z I L

PERU

B O L I V I A

PARAGUAY

A R G E N T I N A

CHILE

URUGUAY

PACIFIC OCEAN

ATLANTIC OCEAN

FALKLAND ISLANDS

City Maps

In big cities, it can be hard to find your way around.

Maps show you many different things about cities. Look at these three city maps.

Some maps of big cities show every single street. These maps are useful for getting around town and finding particular places of interest.

This is a road map of the same place. You can see the whole city and all the major roads running through and around it.

This map doesn't show any streets at all. It shows the route of a railroad that runs under the ground. Look how the lines cross at some stations so that passengers can change trains to go in another direction. How would you get from Cross Street to Old Bridge?

CROSS STREET
HAPPY STREET
CHURCH STREET
CASTLE STREET
BROWN BRIDGE
GREY GATES
NEW ROAD
BROOK STREET
WINTER PLACE
ORANGE STREET
BLUE STREET
LAKE PLACE
WHITE ROAD
ABBEY LANE
MARSH STREET
OLD BRIDGE
POND PLACE
RED ROAD
MILL STREET

OO CHANGEOVER STATION
STATION
EAST LINE
WEST LINE
NORTHERN LINE
CENTRAL LINE

How Maps Are Made

Map drawing is called cartography. Maps have to be **accurate**, or they won't be useful. **Surveyors** work on the ground, measuring distances and gathering information for maps.

Cartographers use these measurements to draw maps on a computer.

Aerial photographs are pictures taken from airplanes in the sky. They show the world from above, just like a map. Aerial photographs are very useful to cartographers.

Satellite photographs are taken from space. They are useful because they show whole countries and **continents**. Can you see Africa in this satellite photograph of the earth?

Atlases

An atlas is a book of maps. This world atlas has maps of every continent, ocean and country in the world. Each page shows a different area.

South-East Australia

Sydney

Adelaide

Canberra

Melbourne

This atlas is open to show part of the country of Australia.

A road atlas shows all the roads in a country. It is very useful for figuring out routes. Some people use a road atlas every day.

Some atlases are about things that happened long ago. Others show where different animals live.

Every place or thing in an atlas is listed in the **index**. The index tells you where to find the place you are looking for.

Special Maps

Can you see what is special about this map? It is called a **relief map**. It shows how high and low the land is. You can see the mountains and plains.

This picture shows how undersea maps are made. Ships use special equipment to measure the depth of the water. This way they can figure out where the hills and valleys are and make a map of the ocean floor.

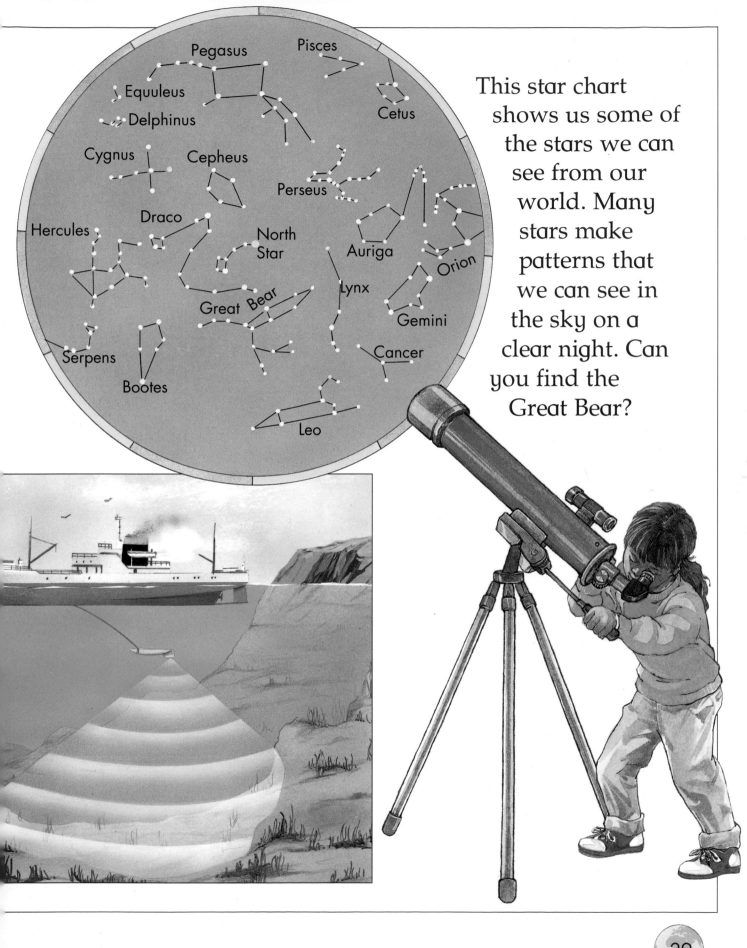

This star chart shows us some of the stars we can see from our world. Many stars make patterns that we can see in the sky on a clear night. Can you find the Great Bear?

Maps and Globes

There is only one way to show the world on a map just as it is in real life. The world is round, and so the map must be round too. These round maps are called globes.

Many maps and globes have **latitude** and **longitude** lines. Just like grids, these lines divide the world into pieces to help people find places.

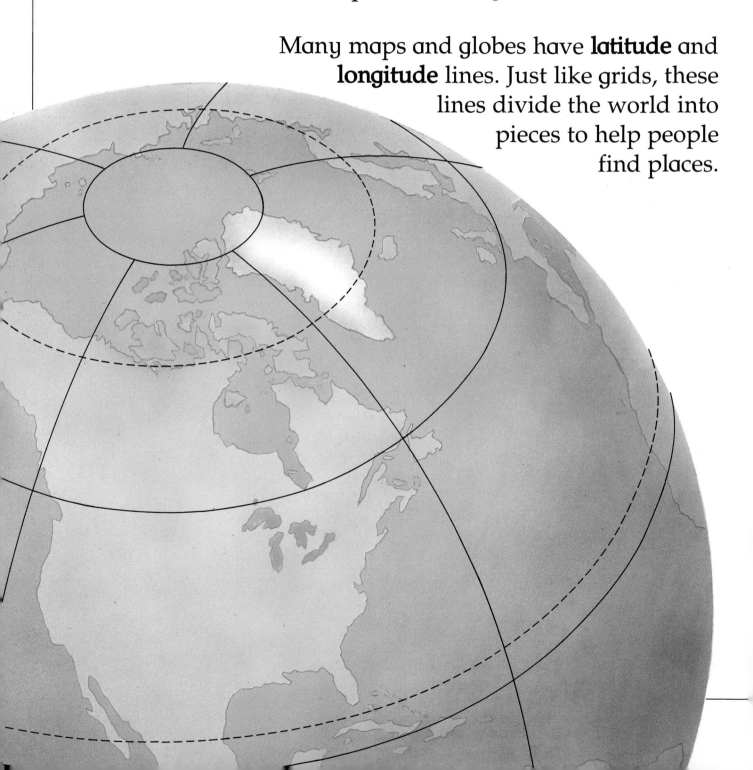

When we go somewhere new, we use a map to find our way. You need a map...

in the town...

in the country...

even indoors!

Without one, you might get lost!

Glossary

Accurate: Free from mistakes

Area: A space, or piece of ground

Boundaries: The limits or borders of an area

Cartographer: A person whose job is to design and draw maps

Compass: A tool used for showing direction

Continents: The main large land areas of the earth

Direction: The way to go to get to a certain point

Distance: The space between two points

Globe: A round model of the world

Grid: A system of lines used for finding places on a map

Index: A list at the end of a book, showing what is in the book and the page it appears on

Latitude: Distance measured north or south of the Equator

Longitude: Distance measured east or west of an imaginary line called the Greenwich Meridian

Plan: A map of a small area

Relief map: A map that shows high and low ground

Route: A road, or way, for traveling

Satellite: A man-made object rocketed into space to go around the earth

Scale: The size of a map in relation to the area it shows

Scale bar: A measured line used for measuring scale

Surveyor: A person whose job is to study and measure areas of land for mapmaking

Index

Aerial photos 24
Africa 25

Boundaries 21

Cartographers 24
Cartography 24
Compass 12

Direction 12-13

Grids 16-17, 30

Index 27

Key 8, 10, 17

Latitude 30
Longitude 30

Relief map 28
Road atlas 26
Road map 23
Route 14

Satellite photos 25
Scale 18-19
South America 21
Star chart 29
Street map 22
Surveyors 24
Symbols 8-9, 11

Tourist map 11
Treasure map 15

Underground map 23

Undersea map 28

Walking map 20
Wildlife atlas 27
World atlas 26

Answers

page 8 The knife-and-fork symbol stands for a restaurant.

page 10 Yellow stands for flower beds and red stands for paths.

page 13 You would have to travel north to get to the mountain. The dog would have to travel east to get back to the farm.

page 17 The pandas are in E1. The sea lions are in D4.

page 23 Route 1: take the East line from Cross Street. Change at Pond Place for the Central line west to Old Bridge. Route 2: take the West line south to Marsh Street. Change to the Northern line up to Winter Place. Change to the Central line for Old Bridge.